D1266033

ARMY
RANGERS

LEE SLATER

Checkerboard Library

An Imprint of Abdo Publishing
abdopublishing.com

abdopublishing.com

Published by Abdo Publishing, a division of ABDO, PO Box 398166, Minneapolis, Minnesota 55439.
Copyright © 2016 by Abdo Consulting Group, Inc. International copyrights reserved in all countries.
No part of this book may be reproduced in any form without written permission from the publisher.
Checkerboard Library™ is a trademark and logo of Abdo Publishing.

Printed in the United States of America, North Mankato, Minnesota
102015
012016

Cover Photo: Teddy Wade/US Army
Interior Photos: Brandon Moreno/US Army, p. 9; Daren Reehl/US Army, p. 14; Herbert Elmer Abrams,
p. 28; Jason T. Bailey/US Army, p. 9; John D. Helms/US Army, p. 20; Michael Lemke/US Department of
the Defense, p. 25; Nathaniel Newkirk/US Army, p. 24; Nikayla Shodeen/US Army, p. 19; Paul Sale/US
Army, p. 18; Pedro Amador/US Army, p. 26; Phil Sussman/US Army, p. 15; Rashene Mincy/US Army,
p. 17; Scott Brooks/US Army, p. 22; Shawn Morris/US Army, p. 9; Steven Hitchcock/US Army, pp. 4, 10,
16, 29; Thomas Hart & Johann Martin Will, pp. 7, 28; US Army, pp. 9, 13, 21, 27, 29; Visual Information
Specialist Gertrud Zach/US Army, p. 12; Wikimedia Commons, pp. 6, 28

Content Developer: Nancy Tuminelly.
Design: Anders Hanson, Mighty Media, Inc.
Editor: Liz Salzmann

Library of Congress Cataloging-in-Publication Data
Slater, Lee, 1969-
 Army Rangers / Lee Slater.
    pages cm. -- (Special ops)
 Includes index.
 ISBN 978-1-62403-967-6
1. United States. Army. Ranger Regiment, 75th--Juvenile literature. 2. United States. Army--
Commando troops--Juvenile literature. I. Title.
 UA34.R36S615 2016
 356'.1670973--dc23
                       2015026584

CONTENTS

TODAY'S RANGERS

Today's Army Rangers are smart, tough, brave, and adventurous. They are strong and capable soldiers, and they don't give up. They are quick thinkers and always ready to take action. Rangers bravely face fear, danger, and unknown obstacles on every mission. They are trained to outsmart and defeat their enemies.

Surprise is one of the Rangers' most effective weapons. To succeed in their missions, Rangers work to discover information about the enemy. This is called intelligence gathering. Rangers learn where the enemy is hiding. Then, they use special skills and equipment to get close to the enemy without being seen.

Rangers are light **infantry** forces that fight on foot. They carry what they need and are in direct combat with the enemy. Rangers often arrive under the cover of darkness. Their enemies are

Rangers wear night vision goggles to see in the dark.

shocked and unable to react quickly enough to defeat the Rangers. Rangers seize and destroy enemy sites and materials, and capture or kill enemies. They also rescue prisoners of war and other people from hostile areas.

Recent Ranger Deployments

1980	Iran, Operation Eagle Claw	1993	Somalia, Operation Gothic Serpent/Restore Hope
1983	Grenada, Operation Urgent Fury		
1989	Panama, Operation Just Cause	2001	Afghanistan, Operation Enduring Freedom
1991	Persian Gulf, Operation Desert Shield/Desert Storm	2003	Iraq, Operation Iraqi Freedom

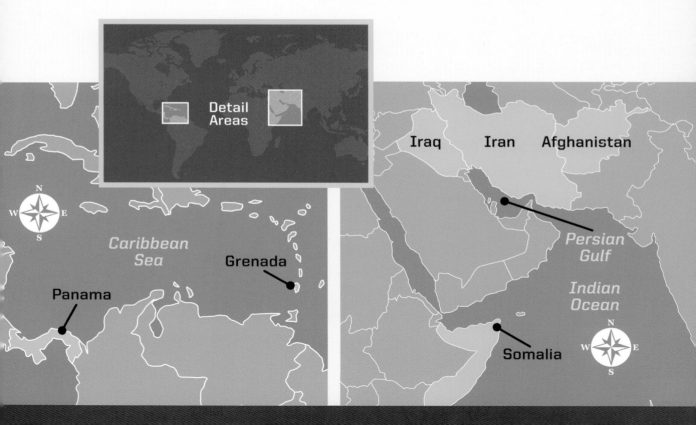

aptain Benjamin Church founded the first American Ranger unit in 1676. They fought in **King Philip's War**. Church's unit copied the way Native Americans fought.

In 1756, Major Robert Rogers created a Ranger unit to fight in the **French and Indian War**. He wrote Standing Orders for the Rangers he commanded. They were rules for how to fight in battle.

Colonel Benjamin Church

Here are some of the rules in Rogers' Standing Orders.

- Don't forget nothing.

- Be ready to march at a minute's warning.

- See the enemy first.

- Tell the truth about what you see and what you do. Don't never lie to a Ranger or officer.

- Don't never take a chance you don't have to.

- When we march, we keep moving till dark.

- Half the party stays awake while the other half sleeps.

- Don't sleep beyond dawn.

- Let the enemy come till he's almost close enough to touch, then let him have it.

Major Robert Rogers

You might notice that Rogers didn't use proper English. For example, he says, "Don't forget nothing" instead of "Don't forget anything." Whether he used proper English or not, his ideas worked. The Standing Orders written by Major Rogers are still included in the *Ranger Handbook*.

The first United States Ranger companies were formed in the early 1800s. The men were frontier settlers. They were used to defending themselves and their land. These Rangers fought in the **War of 1812**. They also acted as scouts and spies, patrolling on foot, horseback, and boat. In the 1860s, Rangers fought in the American **Civil War**.

There weren't any Rangers for a long time after the Civil War. Then during **World War II**, the United States Army activated six Ranger battalions. They fought in all areas of the war, including on the beaches of Normandy, France, on D-Day in 1944. At the end of the war, the Ranger battalions were deactivated. Several Ranger battalions were reactivated to fight in the **Korean War** from 1950 to 1951. Ranger battalions also fought in the **Vietnam War** from 1969 to 1972.

Then, in 1974, the army saw a need for a permanent, highly trained light **infantry** force. To that end, General Creighton Abrams formed the 1st and 2nd Ranger Battalions, 75th Infantry. The 3rd Ranger Battalion was added in 1984. The three battalions were renamed the "75th Ranger Regiment" in 1986. Then, in 2006, the Regimental Special Troops Battalion was activated.

WHAT IS A BATTALION?

A battalion is a large military operational unit. It is made up of smaller units including companies, platoons, and squads.

Squad
4-10 soldiers

Platoon
(3-4 squads) 16-40 soldiers

Company
(3-4 platoons) 100-200 soldiers

Battalion
(3-5 companies) 500-600 soldiers

CHAPTER 4

WORDS THAT
RANGERS
LIVE BY

A creed is a set of beliefs or principles shared by a group. Every member agrees to the creed and promises to follow it. The Ranger Creed has six parts. The first letter of each part spells "RANGER."

THE RANGER CREED

RECOGNIZING that I volunteered as a Ranger, fully knowing the **hazards** of my chosen profession, I will always endeavor to **uphold** the **prestige**, honor, and high **esprit de corps** of my Ranger Regiment.

ACKNOWLEDGING the fact that a Ranger is a more **elite** soldier, who arrives at the cutting edge of battle by land, sea, or air, I accept the fact that as a Ranger, my country expects me to move further, faster, and fight harder than any other soldier.

NEVER shall I fail my comrades. I will always keep myself mentally alert, physically strong, and morally straight, and I will shoulder more than my share of the task, whatever it may be, one hundred percent and then some.

GALLANTLY will I show the world that I am a specially selected and well-trained soldier. My courtesy to superior officers, neatness of dress, and care of equipment shall set the example for others to follow.

ENERGETICALLY will I meet the enemies of my country. I shall defeat them on the field of battle for I am better trained and will fight with all my might. Surrender is not a Ranger word. I will never leave a fallen comrade to fall into the hands of the enemy and under no **circumstances** will I ever embarrass my country.

READILY will I display the intestinal **fortitude** required to fight on to the Ranger objective and complete the mission, though I be the lone survivor. Since 1944, the Ranger **motto** has been "Rangers Lead the Way."

BECOMING
A RANGER

The 75th Ranger Regiment looks for smart, strong, committed soldiers. A Ranger candidate shows his commitment by volunteering three times. First, he volunteers to serve in the army. Second, he volunteers for Airborne School. Third, he volunteers by requesting assignment to the 75th Ranger Regiment.

A soldier does sit-ups during the physical fitness test.

Any **enlisted** soldier or officer who meets the following qualifications can volunteer to become a Ranger.

- is male
- is a US citizen
- is on active duty and volunteers for the assignment
- earns a passing General Technical Score
- earns a passing Physical Training Score
- has no physical limitations
- qualifies and volunteers for Airborne School
- is a person of good character
- has or enlists into a Military **Occupational** Specialty found in the 75th Ranger Regiment
- is able to get at least a Secret clearance

The physical fitness test also includes push-ups.

Candidates go through Ranger **Assessment** and Selection Program (RASP). RASP has two levels. RASP 1 is for junior **non-commissioned officers** and **enlisted** soldiers. RASP 2 is for senior non-commissioned officers, officers, and warrant officers.

RASP 1 is an eight-week course. During the course, the candidates learn the basics of what it takes to be a Ranger. They are tested on their mental and physical capabilities. The candidates also learn the advanced skills all Rangers are required to master. They learn fighting methods, **marksmanship**, medical skills, and physical fitness.

RASP 2 is a three-week course. Like in RASP 1, the candidates are tested on their physical and mental capabilities. They also learn the special skills and processes that set the Ranger Regiment apart. In addition, they study what will be expected of them as officers. Ranger officers need to know how to effectively lead the men in their units.

Regardless of the course, candidates must meet the course requirements in order to become Army Rangers. Only then will they receive Ranger tan **berets** and 75th Ranger Regiment Scrolls.

A Ranger practices shooting a moving target.

RASP REQUIREMENTS

- Score at least 240 on the Army Physical Fitness Test and be able to do six pull-ups.
- Run 5 miles (8 km) in 40 minutes.
- March 12 miles (19 km) in 3 hours while carrying 35 pounds (16 kg).
- Complete the Ranger Swim Ability **Evaluation**.
- Pass a mental screening.
- RASP 1 candidates must pass security screening and receive a SECRET clearance. RASP 2 candidates must have at least an Interim SECRET clearance before starting RASP.
- Pass the Commander's Board. For RASP 1 candidates this event is for select individuals based on peer evaluations, instructor **assessment**, and overall performance. The Commander's Board is a requirement for all RASP 2 candidates.
- RASP 1 candidates must successfully complete the RASP 1 Program of Instruction.

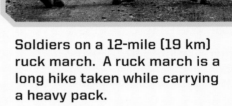

Soldiers on a 12-mile (19 km) ruck march. A ruck march is a long hike taken while carrying a heavy pack.

THE RANGER HANDBOOK

Every US Army Ranger receives a copy of the *Ranger Handbook*. It is a training tool and a reference book. The *Ranger Handbook* starts with the Ranger Creed and Major Rogers' Standing Orders. Then there is a section on the history of the Rangers.

The rest of the handbook covers practically everything a Ranger needs to know to do his job. Topics range from leading a patrol to escaping from the enemy to first aid. It includes diagrams for setting up a communications antenna, for planning an **ambush**, and much more.

Rangers on patrol sneak up on a target.

Many Rangers bring it on every mission. Some soldiers put clear plastic over the covers to protect them from water damage. The *Ranger Handbook* is often referred to as the Ranger bible.

Two Rangers fire a recoilless rifle. The *Ranger Handbook* covers how and when to use various weapons.

US ARMY
RANGER SCHOOL

Ranger School is the army's top leadership school. It is one of the toughest military training courses in existence. In spite of the name, Ranger School is not directly connected to the 75th Ranger Regiment. Soldiers from all branches of the military can go to Ranger School. Completing it is not required to become an Army Ranger. However, it is required for Army Ranger officers ranking sergeant or higher. Ranger school has three **phases**.

Ranger School students train in all weather conditions.

THE BENNING PHASE

The first **phase** of Ranger School is the Benning phase. It takes place at Fort Benning, Georgia. The Benning phase starts with the Ranger **assessment** phase, known as "RAP week." RAP week is four days of demanding physical tests and mental challenges. It also includes navigation, weapons, and communications training.

Students tackle an obstacle on the Darby Queen obstacle course.

After RAP week comes the patrol phase, also called "Darby phase." It covers leading troops, patrolling, **demolitions**, and basic battle drills. Students also have to complete the Darby Queen obstacle course. It has 20 obstacles spread over uneven, hilly land.

Students spend the rest of the Benning phase conducting patrols. Each student must show he can plan, prepare, and lead a combat patrol. He not only has to prove himself to the instructors, but also to his fellow students. There is a peer **evaluation** that is part of each student's score.

THE MOUNTAIN PHASE

The second **phase** of Ranger School is the mountain phase. It is located at Camp Frank D. Merrill in the northern Georgia mountains. The candidates learn military mountaineering and new combat methods. They learn about knots, ropes, climbing, **rappelling**, and mountain survival. The training missions include patrols, **ambushes**, **raids**, river crossings, and mountain climbing. Candidates take turns leading patrols so that everyone gains leadership skills.

Students rappel down a cliff during the mountain phase.

THE FLORIDA PHASE

The third **phase** of Ranger School is the Florida phase. It takes place at Camp James E. Rudder, Florida. The students practice patrols and operations on land, in the water, and from the air. They experience extreme mental and physical stress. They learn how to survive in swamps and jungles. In the final 10 days, the training exercises include realistic **raids**, **ambushes**, and assaults. To complete this phase, the students have to apply everything they have learned. Ranger School graduates receive a Ranger tab to wear on their uniforms.

FEMALE RANGERS

In 2015, women were allowed to attend Ranger School for the first time in history. On August 21, Captain Kristen Griest and First Lieutenant Shaye Haver became the first female soldiers to graduate from the course. Griest and Haver will receive a Ranger tab to wear on their uniforms. However, they cannot join the 75th Ranger Regiment. So far, the military does not allow women to become active combat Rangers.

Every Ranger will be **deployed** on a mission at some time. Rangers are always ready to go. They know they can be deployed without any warning. When a Ranger is not on a mission, he is still on duty at the base.

Every Ranger has a Military **Occupational** Specialty. That means he has training in a skill the army needs. Some of these specialties are jobs found outside the military too. They include construction, food service, accounting, health care, and transportation. Other specialties are military-specific jobs, such as command sergeant major, combat engineer, and **infantryman**. Rangers can also attend classes to improve their job skills. They can take classes at military or non-military schools.

Ranger training never stops. Rangers need to keep their fighting skills sharp and their bodies fit. They never know when the order for deployment will come.

Rangers maintain their skills with live fire training.

WHERE TO FIND ARMY RANGERS

2ND BATTALION, 75TH RANGER REGIMENT, FORT LEWIS, WASHINGTON

1ST BATTALION, 75TH RANGER REGIMENT, HUNTER ARMY AIRFIELD, GEORGIA

REGIMENTAL SPECIAL TROOPS BATTALION, FORT BENNING, GEORGIA

3RD BATTALION, 75TH RANGER REGIMENT, FORT BENNING, GEORGIA

TOOLS
OF THE TRADE

Army Rangers travel light. They are usually on foot. They fight in close combat situations. They need to be able to move quickly without being seen.

Rangers carry personal weapons, such as a pistol, rifle, and knife. They also carry **ammunition**, survival supplies, and a medical kit. Rangers are resourceful and they often adapt weapons to suit their needs.

Rangers fire a 120mm mortar.
A mortar is a type of cannon.

Besides their pistols and rifles, Rangers use machine guns, **grenade** launchers, mortars, and antitank weapons.

Rangers also use explosives. They use them to break down and open fences, gates, and walls. Some explosives are large and hard to transport on foot. Rangers prefer to carry raw materials and assemble the charge where it is needed.

US Army Land Rover Defender Multi Role Combat Vehicle (MRCV)

Army Rangers use several types of vehicles. Two of them are the Multi Role Combat Vehicle (MRCV) and the Special Operations Vehicle (SOV). These vehicles can be fitted with machine guns and grenade launchers. They are used for fighting and scouting, as well as carrying soldiers and gear. Modified versions of them are used to transport soldiers who are wounded.

THE FUTURE
OF THE RANGERS

Today's Rangers are constantly active in combat operations. They are **deployed** alongside other forces in Iraq and Afghanistan. They perform missions including airborne and air assaults, and **raids** in enemy territory. They also perform rescue missions.

Rangers in Afghanistan wait to be picked up by a CH-47 helicopter.

A Ranger on lookout in Iraq

The Rangers continue to train in the United States and overseas. They are prepared to **deploy** on short notice for any future combat missions. The 75th Regiment is always looking for new volunteers. The next generation of Rangers and Ranger leaders needs to be ready when called to duty. Whatever the future holds, the US Army Rangers will always be ready. And when it's time for action, the Rangers will lead the way.

TIMELINE

1676
Colonel Benjamin Church founds the first American Ranger unit.

1944
Rangers land on the Normandy beaches on D-Day.

1984
The 3rd Ranger Battalion, 75th Infantry, is formed.

1756
Major Robert Rogers creates a Ranger unit to fight in the French and Indian War.

1812
Rangers fight in the War of 1812.

1974
General Creighton Abrams forms the 1st and 2nd Ranger Battalions, 75th Infantry.

1986

The Ranger Battalions, 75th Infantry, are renamed the "75th Ranger Regiment."

2006

the Regimental Special Troops Battalion is activated.

EXTREME FACTS

- Many famous men have been Rangers, including Abraham Lincoln and Daniel Boone.

- The Rangers are among a very few units that have been constantly **deployed** since 9/11.

- During the **Korean War** the 2nd Ranger Company was an all African-American Ranger company.

- The Best Ranger Competition takes place every year at Fort Benning, Georgia.

- The Ranger Monument is one of the most visited sites at Fort Benning. It is a tribute to the service and sacrifice of the US Army Rangers.

GLOSSARY

ambush – a surprise attack from a hidden position.

ammunition – bullets, shells, cartridges, or other items used in firearms.

assessment – a decision about how good or bad something is.

beret – a soft, flat cap that does not have a brim.

circumstance – the condition at a certain place or time.

civil war – a war between groups in the same country. The United States of America and the Confederate States of America fought a civil war from 1861 to 1865.

demolition – the act of destroying something, especially by using explosives.

deploy – to spread out and organize in a battle formation.

elite – of or relating to the best of a class.

enlist – to join the armed forces voluntarily. An enlisted man is a person who enlists for military service.

esprit de corps – a French term for feelings of loyalty and trust among members of a group.

evaluation – a decision about how good or bad something is.

fortitude – strength of mind that helps someone face danger or pain with courage.

French and Indian War – a war fought from 1754 to 1763 between French and British settlers in the American colonies.

grenade – a small bomb that is thrown by hand or shot from a gun.

hazard – a source of danger.

infantry – soldiers trained and organized to fight on foot. An infantry soldier is called an infantryman.

WEBSITES

To learn more about Special Ops, visit **booklinks.abdopublishing.com**. These links are routinely monitored and updated to provide the most current information available.

King Philip's War – a war fought from 1675 to 1676. It took place in New England between English settlers and Native Americans.

Korean War – a war fought in North and South Korea from 1950 to 1953. The US government sent troops to help South Korea.

marksmanship – the skill of shooting a target.

motto – a word or sentence that describes a guiding principle.

non-commissioned officer – an officer who started as an enlisted soldier and was promoted to officer.

occupational – related to a job or profession.

phase – a step or stage of a process.

prestige – being thought of as important by other people.

raid – a surprise attack.

rappel – to lower oneself down a rope, often from a cliff or a helicopter.

uphold – to support something you believe to be right.

Vietnam War – from 1957 to 1975. A long, failed attempt by the United States to stop North Vietnam from taking over South Vietnam.

War of 1812 – from 1812 to 1814. A war fought between the United States and the United Kingdom over shipping rights and the capture of US seamen.

World War II – from 1939 to 1945, fought in Europe, Asia, and Africa. Great Britain, France, the United States, the Soviet Union, and their allies were on one side. Germany, Italy, Japan, and their allies were on the other side.

INDEX